D0623266

SHARK FRENZY

Blue Sharks

by Thomas K. Adamson

BELLWETHER MEDIA • MINNEAPOLIS, MN

Blastoff! Readers are carefully developed by literacy experts to build reading stamina and move students toward fluency by combining standards-based content with developmentally appropriate text.

Level 1 provides the most support through repetition of high-frequency words, light text, predictable sentence patterns, and strong visual support.

Level 2 offers early readers a bit more challenge through varied sentences, increased text load, and text-supportive special features.

Level 3 advances early-fluent readers toward fluency through increased text load, less reliance on photos, advancing concepts, longer sentences, and more complex special features.

★ **Blastoff! Universe**

Reading Level

Grade **K**

Grades **1–3**

Grade **4**

This edition first published in 2021 by Bellwether Media, Inc.

No part of this publication may be reproduced in whole or in part without written permission of the publisher. For information regarding permission, write to Bellwether Media, Inc., Attention: Permissions Department, 6012 Blue Circle Drive, Minnetonka, MN 55343.

Library of Congress Cataloging-in-Publication Data

Names: Adamson, Thomas K., 1970- author.
Title: Blue sharks / by Thomas K. Adamson.
Description: Minneapolis, MN : Bellwether Media, [2021] | Series: Blastoff! Readers: Shark frenzy | Includes bibliographical references and index. | Audience: Ages 5-8 | Audience: Grades 2-3 | Summary: "Simple text and full-color photography introduce beginning readers to blue sharks. Developed by literacy experts for students in kindergarten through third grade"-Provided by publisher.
Identifiers: LCCN 2020001607 (print) | LCCN 2020001608 (ebook) | ISBN 9781644872444 (library binding) | ISBN 9781681037073 (ebook)
Subjects: LCSH: Blue sharks–Juvenile literature.
Classification: LCC QL638.95.C3 A33 2021 (print) | LCC QL638.95.C3 (ebook) | DDC 597.3/4–dc23
LC record available at https://lccn.loc.gov/2020001607
LC ebook record available at https://lccn.loc.gov/2020001608

Editor: Rebecca Sabelko   Designer: Kathleen Petelinsek

Printed in the United States of America, North Mankato, MN.

Table of Contents

Blue sharks are open-ocean swimmers found all around the world! They live in both warm and cool waters.

These sharks are known for their bright blue color. This striking color is how they got their name!

Blue Shark Range

N
W ✦ E
S

range = ☐

Blue sharks are **near threatened**. They are often **snagged** in fishing nets. Many are fished just for their fins.

Some countries now ban **finning**. People work to **conserve** these powerful sharks!

Blue sharks have **camouflage** called **countershading**. Their blue backs look like the ocean water when seen from above.

From below, their white bellies look like the light-colored surface.

pectoral fin

Blue sharks are made to ride ocean **currents**. They can easily swim across the ocean!

Their thin bodies stretch up to 13 feet (4 meters) long. Their **pectoral fins** are long and pointed.

Shark Sizes

☐ average human   ☐ blue shark

6 feet (2 meters) long •--

up to 13 feet (4 meters) long •--

Blue sharks have large, round eyes.

Identify a Blue Shark

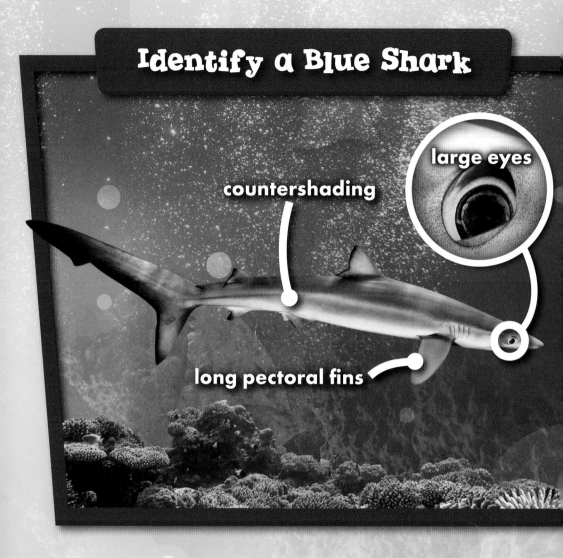

large eyes

countershading

long pectoral fins

Their eyes allow them to see changes in light underwater. This helps the sharks hunt at night. They can easily see moving **prey**.

Open-ocean Hunters

Blue sharks **migrate** long distances when waters get too warm.

They also travel to follow food. These hunters make many trips across the ocean in their lifetimes!

school of fish

Blue sharks follow large **schools** of small fish. This lets the sharks eat a lot at one time.

Blue sharks also eat octopuses, seabirds, and dead whales. They often dive into deep waters to find their prey.

Blue Shark Diet

octopuses

seabirds

small fish

Blue sharks do not have many **predators**. But they have to watch out for larger sharks and **orcas**. People are also a threat.

These beautiful blue sharks
are always on the lookout!

Deep Dive on the Blue Shark

LIFE SPAN:
up to 20 years

LENGTH:
up to 13 feet (4 meters) long

WEIGHT:
more than 520 pounds
(236 kilograms)

TOP SPEED:
25 miles (40 kilometers) per hour

countershading

long
pectoral fins

large eyes

Least Concern	Near Threatened	Vulnerable	Endangered	Critically Endangered	Extinct in the Wild	Extinct

conservation status: near threatened

21

Glossary

camouflage—a way of using color to blend in with surroundings

conserve—to keep safe

countershading—a type of coloring in which the top of the body is darker than the lower parts of the body; countershading is a type of camouflage.

currents—patterns of water movement in a body of water

finning—removing a shark's fins and returning the rest of the shark to the ocean

migrate—to move from one area to another, often with the seasons

near threatened—may become extinct in the near future

orcas—killer whales

pectoral fins—a pair of fins on the side of a shark that control a shark's movement

predators—animals that hunt other animals for food

prey—animals that are hunted by other animals for food

schools—groups of fish

snagged—to get caught by something or someone

To Learn More

AT THE LIBRARY

Adamson, Thomas K. *Great White Sharks*. Minneapolis, Minn.: Bellwether Media, 2021.

Dempski, Seth. *In Search of Blue Sharks*. New York, N.Y.: PowerKids Press, 2016.

Skerry, Brian. *The Ultimate Book of Sharks: Your Guide to These Fierce and Fantasic Fish*. Washington, D.C.: National Geographic, 2018.

ON THE WEB

FACTSURFER

Factsurfer.com gives you a safe, fun way to find more information.

1. Go to www.factsurfer.com.

2. Enter "blue sharks" into the search box and click 🔍.

3. Select your book cover to see a list of related content.

Index

The images in this book are reproduced through the courtesy of: Joost van Uffelen, front cover; wildestanimal, pp. 3, 4-5; National Geographic Image Collection/ Alamy, pp. 6-7; Alessandro De Maddalena, p. 7; Pommeyrol Vincent, p. 8; Martin Prochazkacz, pp. 9, 10-11, 12, 13 (large eyes), 21 (large eyes); Fiona Ayerst, pp. 13 (blue shark), 23; Chris & Monique Fallows/ OceanWideImages, pp. 14-15; Cultura Creative (RF)/ Alamy, p. 15; Nature Picture Library/ Alamy, pp. 16-17, 18; Chris Gug/ Alamy, p. 17 (octopuses); Andrew M. Allport, p. 17 (seabirds); Stephen Frink Collection/ Alamy, p. 17 (small fish); annalisa e marina duante, pp. 18-19; Marion Kraschl, pp. 20-21.